Gallery Books
Editor Peter Fallon
LONG DISTANCE

John FitzGerald

LONG DISTANCE

Gallery Books

Long Distance
is first published
simultaneously in paperback
and in a clothbound edition
on 18 April 2024.

The Gallery Press
Loughcrew
Oldcastle
County Meath
Ireland

www.gallerypress.com

*All rights reserved. For permission
to reprint or broadcast these poems,
write to The Gallery Press:*
books@gallerypress.com

© John FitzGerald 2024

The right of John FitzGerald to be identified as Author of this Work has been asserted in accordance with Section 77 of the Copyright, Designs and Patents Act 1988.

ISBN 978 1 91133 880 2 *paperback*
    978 1 91133 881 9 *clothbound*

A CIP catalogue record for this book
is available from the British Library.

Long Distance receives financial assistance
from the Arts Council.

Contents

Familiar *page* 11
Clanrath 12
Deor 13
American Woodcock 14
Windfall Stars 15
'Back from a night cycle...' 18
Made Strange 19
Egret at Key West 20
Keats in Belfast 21
Revenant 22
Lauriston 23
Nursery Rhymes 24
Drop Off 26
Wounded Angel 27
Thornflower 28
Discovering Kerry 29
Return to Coolea 30
Boulevard du Temple, 1838 32
Blueprints 33
Message 34
Before You Speak 36
Magnus Modus 38
Grus Grus 39
Haiku na Feirme 40
The Nightjar 44
Encroachment 46
At Sea 47
After Ælfric
   1 A MAN OF WINCHESTER 48
   2 THE SPIRIT IS BY NATURE A TRINITY 48
   3 LET US NOW CONSIDER THE SWIFTNESS OF SPIRIT 49
Dan 50
'The May Altar...' 51
Lost Chorus 52
Long Distance 53
Crex Crex 54

Working from Home 55
Dreaming Seamus Heaney
   1 A BAR OUT WEST 56
   2 THE EAST WING 56
   3 THE LONG HALL 57
   4 A READING IN DUBLIN 57
   5 STRANGE WORDS 58
   6 DELICATESSE 58
   7 THE FACE 59
Steeplechase 60
Vixen 61
Anything 62
Interval 63
Solstice 64
Oriole 65
Strobus 66
Artisan 67
The Miller 68
Athairne 69
Haus Sonas 70
Byrd 71
Excursion 72
Such a Thing 74
Our Journey 75
On McAllister Street 76
Caption 77
Afforestation 78
On Reaching Heng Mountain 79

Acknowledgements and Notes 81

for Róisín

Familiar

She watches with her whole body,
muscles and skin
sensing our precise distance,
eyes wide to everything.

The wood is still,
a few phases of wind
through leaves and ferns,
the bluebells' silent ringing.

Staring intently she lifts a shoulder,
leg, angles towards me slowly,
ears like felt periscopes,
every nerve bow-taut, ready to fly.

And then I realize
I am the one being stalked: this is you,
your faded coat, hint of age in your hair,
your watchful reticence
and wanting always to be away.

Clanrath

Now that you are dead I can write this.
Even if I never did call in to climb

your hill and see the famous view.
I kept your secret all these years,

from that lonesome place
where I thought I'd not encounter anyone,

going there to forget the cities
I had lately been in. Only to meet you two

walking from the trees
so plainly having been together.

Our awkward glance, her downward stare,
fair complexion, a scene engraved

by memory in all its detail. And after,
a reason for our distance, until

we both became relaxed with age
such that, I think, it didn't matter much.

Before she died I visited your wife
in her sparse parlour. The bindweed

on the lane was cruelly sensual,
shot through with streaks of pink.

Deor

Stonemasons are straight talkers too.
Nothing lasts, he says, packing the pocket
between girder and blocks with gravelly muck.

Good and bad, nothing. The only good thing
about the bad stuff is that it won't last.

He flings a damp slob on the new block,
slices and dices it, scoops it up,
then spreads it fast to take the next course.

A high, light-filled lecture hall,
desktop pitted with names and dates,
Deor inked across the opened page.

Your gates, my pillars, this place. All gone
sooner or later, d'you get what I'm saying?

American Woodcock

My flight path over Fortitude and Patience
brought me into
these amazing glass canyons,

an arrow with Athena's agility
channelling the strength of Atlas,
until tonight —

the Morgan Stanley Building
came in the way and I dwindled
to the sidewalk, a spent oil-can

its ruddy glob on the nib of my beak.
Look. That's me there,
dead on the warm concrete.

Windfall Stars

Wet with rain
these power lines shine in the sun
like silver skeins linking

a dilemma. Stand beneath them
and they hum and buzz
or fizzle in a lint of starlings.

They scar but — like all
our useful engineering — less the more
they meet our need and want.

No Pylons Here on faded
boards along the road. Beyond,
a victory march of masts

pivots at a steel erection.
I track them back to Cloontycarty
where giant reapers

harvest wind for our new
eco-elixir. Once a favoured
stopping point, habitat

of harrier and grouse,
now a dwarfing steel
and concrete spinney

cordoned off to guard
its fragile economics. They stand
aloof like outsize sentinels,

their rising plunging arms
unsynchronized — yet
united by proportion

and the slow motion of their winding.
Poor things, they'd make it
into flight given the least uplift.

Up close, the heave and sigh
of routine labour
as passing air is sliced and served

and fed into an underworld
rewired. Giant triffids,
Scylla and Charybdis combined,

each the girth of a lighthouse
sniffing out and snubbing noses
at the prevailing wind,

three-armed engines standing
ever ready to turn, turn
so that we may be warm,

the sick can heal, factories
will make the things we need.
O great white triskelions,

beacons of hope, your bright
pilot lights shining, you could well
be our New Age Ariadne

or a last foolish throw of the dice;
visible for miles, you have
redrawn our horizons, defiled

sacred stations, and yet we can
no longer resist your proliferation
or the benefit of your industry.

Even the moon rising in the east
has become collateral
to your grounded supremacy.

The hills around me darken
and soon the valleys fill
with windfall stars — light and heat

for grateful families and farms,
some gifted young physicist
or bioengineer out there

broaching a first discovery.
I walk back to the car
out of step with each slow cut

into the darkness behind.
Back home again, unsure
of what to do about our future

here on Earth, the kettle smokes,
my laptop glows, these
lines fill the screen.

'*Back from a night cycle . . .*'

he brought me out to see the sky
as if he had just invented it, pointing
out the pan angled for a drip to drop,
the spray paint of the Milky Way
and how the Pleiades are clearer — don't! —
when you look askance. I'll be going to parties
more now, he said, in cars with lads,
driving a tractor maybe next year. He didn't
wait for my reply. He alone had made this sky,
its velvet deep, its endless interstices,
and in the busy workshop of his mind
had built a future too, out of the bits
and pieces of his days and dreams
and some, borrowed without asking, of mine.

Made Strange

The song his flung stick sings
as it spins across the ice
is lunar, sonar, radio-magnetic,

gliding impossibly out
beyond the middle of the lake —
so still and clear down there

where the encased water
seems replaced by air.

He reads the sound,
figures out its message
much better than I —

the references in his angled head
bringing him to smile
as he orchestrates each one

into a new interpretation
of everything he knows
and every known thing.

Egret at Key West

Straight out of Audubon
or an avian catwalk

into a world given over
to cockerels, fish houses,
rough men of the sea,

your measured process
along the sidewalk —

each leg lifted and held
and set down,
step by deliberate step,

eyes straight ahead
ignoring everything,
but your deity.

Keats in Belfast

We did little to lift your gloom
(if only it could have stopped raining),

the shock to your system
of Duchess Dunghill training

her *skinny lidded inanity*
on you; unfortunate aisling.

Nothing either to ease
your ears of the throttling

fervour of the looms.
Even Ailsa Rock made game

after of your fragile state,
your world in a hames.

Revenant

I craved your stare, your touch,
the thrill of your fingers on the back of my hand,
the point just inside the rim of your pupil —
a blue translucence keeping your consuming
obsession with thin-wafer technology
from my aching hopeless mess of a world.
Cropped hair the colour of pith,
your torso taut above the rocking waves,
you wore my speckled jumper threadbare.
Knuckles white after rain around a coffee mug.
Your lack of any capacity for love never bothered me,
but why, forty years later,
have you returned to ask me back —
a chance encounter outside your flat, tea,
the unmade bed? As if any of this ever mattered.

Lauriston

Who lives in Lauriston, the house in the park,
on the Mardyke, behind old railings and hedging?
Is it the Park Keeper?
Or a city father?
Or some professor emeritus?
I must know who lives in Lauriston,
who chose that eggshell blue,
planted up the pots by the door,
neglects to repair the chimney stack,
savours the shade and seclusion
from all who pass so close by.
Who lives in Lauriston? I asked as I passed —
we all need to know who have ever wondered
at what we cannot see but imagine concretely.
Who lives in Lauriston? a voice replied,
but it was mine answering me,
thirty years later.

Nursery Rhymes

1

Something about the future when my
namesake ran his bright lascivious eye
over the place — the deeds say '94 —
and put his maidens down we think before
the house had started. Seven rows of eight
by all accounts as exquisite in taste
as blossom. A dozen survived to me —
one handful of desserts, six tart Bramleys
and a dual-purpose Sheep's Snout, by far
our best cropper and ornamental star.
Just as there comes a time to pick the fruit
so too to propagate and follow suit —
bury the rootstock, be sure to nourish
and tend the ground for the plants to flourish.

2

The perfect site, south facing, slight incline
for our new orchard, the last past its prime.
Find native varieties we were told
better to resist and not break the mould —
try Dick Davies and a Rawley's Seedling,
Ard Cairn Russet, Ballinora Pippin,
all locally sourced, and without the need
to expropriate their locality.
Then two more came by post as birthday gifts
(the brazen confidence of colonists),
a Jonagold and a Beauty of Bath,
both upscuttling our applecart —
yet reminding us too of who we were:
variety? it's all about *terroir*.

3

They seem to grow in spite of me these days,
lay down subterranean canopies
to mine the soil for sustenance and hold
while slender branches like forearms unfold,
slim girths expand, leaves finger light and air,
apparet! they thrive best without my care,
neglecting to weed them and prune them back,
inspect for canker or fruit-fly attack.
And if they too make it to middle age —
by which time I'll be approaching the edge
of the unknown, who might graft again
and where will they preserve our strains?
Out there, I should be pleased if just one tree
grows not in spite of, but instead of me.

Drop Off

Afterwards I feared it often;
still do.

Will check always
for cuff or coattail snagged in a jamb.

They put it down to age and drink —
two old-timers,

their loud goodnights
like chapel chimes,

his red Toyota springing
along the boreen

dragging what was left
into the yard.

Wounded Angel

Limbs crackling, sudden leaf-crash —
a cloud hurled to the ground, a blowaway
sheet, feathered, rolling to our feet.
Out here for fish and fire, boy-wildness,
and now this bird-thing appears,
moss and flowers clung to what's not
cotton or gauze — more like bleached
wasp-paper or dried lake-froth. The eyes
turning to us, face zagged with blood: it is
the watery eyes that speak first — then
the gawping mouth, in faint roosting calls.
We cut two poles, strap them with bark,
bind her head. Ruined it, she has, tripping
all the way home on that damned shawl.

Thornflower

These weavers who steal into fields
at night to stitch bright tapestry
on trees, the fields become galleries,
arcades, each one decked
in their cover and spread: who are they?
Never unsettling the stock or blurring
the scutch or flighting our owl.

Stray émigrés of Gobelins?
Their tenders idling, their fires
doused before dawn, their scent
dispelling behind them?
We fete all May in whose mastery,
eyes lifted, hearts filled
by the generous glint, the heedless dazzle.

Discovering Kerry

I'd come at a bad time — you would explain later —
but even half-welcome

was better than my desolation
at home alone in the middle of summer.

Two bikes against the hall wall
would deliver us into the estate, lakes, woodland;

we even made it up the Long Range
to Lord Brandon's Cottage,

as un-Black Valley as I could have imagined.
From there, through the Gap, all the way

down and out to Beaufort — for fondue.
On the bus home across the County Bounds,

or maybe via Rathmore,
the driver whistled 'The Banks of Sullane'.

Return to Coolea

It didn't seem strange, the whole school
facing the passing traffic on our knees —
we knelt in ignorance often. But our

sudden hush surprised us when a hearse
appeared on Cork Street by the FCA.
A hundred heads tracked its steady crawl,

the engine's soft percussion,
teachers and brothers genuflecting
at the drop of gear in salutation.

We watched a dumbshow of pale faces
leaning forward, back, as they looked out at us
through cloud-reflecting glass.

Ruth stared from a black lace mantilla,
her darker eyes piercing mine:
I had not known such beautiful sorrow.

Behind her, among the smaller figures
that stiffened at our gaze, you Peadar
though badly wounded, no doubt defiant,

your lip set in determined abrogation
already unmaking all this.
Now, forty years on,

ten years older than Seán was then,
I pass your house behind its veil of greenery.
No spectators here, no *'Here once lived . . .'*

just a family home, welcoming porch,
sheltered eaves, *luibhghort* by the gable,
love's heroics well hidden inside.

Farther up the hill,
as day gives way to evening,
I leave the road for a last look north and west.

Briars, disturbed, settle back into place.
A line of cattle tracks the slope towards cover,
unstitching the damp grass.

The wind drops, and from the churchyard
wood below come faint discordant notes
of bass male voices still in proud lament.

Boulevard du Temple, 1838

You'll see in Daguerre's vacant streetscape
tall chimney pots, a slanted downpipe,
trees in various states — everything
you'd miss glancing at the landing window
for the umpteenth time. But why here?
The closest point of proof? Humanity
at its best? And yet, the shutter on delay
to catch sufficient light has lost all signs
of passing life: the horses, buses, people —
all gone, but for one, whose stillness
tricked and tripped up Time, stopped
to have his boots shone — a small allowable
indulgence — leaning on his stick,
killing time as it immortalizes him.

Blueprints

1

Even the constellations are versative.
Tonight we mistook the twin heads of Gemini
peering over the western horizon for the Crab.
And, then, crabs' eyes everywhere:
aslant, at right angle, one asquint —
until we realized it was a crawling satellite,
a *sky-louse,* you said.

The moon visible only in the sea,
its light glowing and fading in slow pulses,
as though rehearsing an appearance.
Hercules in the south, rangy and brave as an anchor.

2

Stripping the wallpaper from an upstairs room
I was surprised to encounter
a forgotten signet of my childhood —
and that it was still there.

I had lived eye-to-eye with this pastel miniature
from earliest memory:
a colourfully dressed infant troupe
set against pale blue air, playing on lutes and timbrels
as they walked an invisible path,
umpteen identical knots on diagonals along the walls,

the particular group by the head of my bed,
where I would usually wake turned in,
though similar to all the others,
their tiny faces, and the larger one they made,
still as familiar and strange.

Message

Since you left
I've been tracking the clocks' gongs
as they gather and align and fall
awry again.

I curate nightly
the hall fire from a blaze
of coal and oak to a grate
of cinders and ash,

observe frost grow on glass
in glittering fronds,
then melt to mist
at first light.

I've been talking
to the dogs,
consorting with horses,

going shoulder to shoulder
into stiff winds
with the last of the solitary bees.

I hear engines labouring up the yard,
a clink of gates,
crunching on the gravel
when there's nothing.

How do you feel?
What do you see and hear?
Are your lines still as pure
as contrails across blue sky?

This morning
that shake on your breath
in the message you left.

Before You Speak

Your love is lust
even before you speak,

even as our eyes meet
and we sense

an unevenness that
our hands anticipate,

our attitudes seek
to settle somewhere

in the other's tense
*un*tensioning — until

we both give in
to the old mystique

of fading breathless
reticence.

It is the knowing
what will happen now

that we've signalled
our release,

the slow capitulation
to what endless

dreams can't give —
the drawing each

into the other
where you can turn

your love to lust,
your lust to love.

Magnus Modus

Moments of success the most dangerous,
this is cliff edge stuff, your apotheosis, stem,
rib and ribbon, a twist fused in time, pure

movement, a smooth buckle engrained
with ages of strain, a stream ended
and upturned, a fountain forestalled and folded.

Division is equal, flourishing into itself,
a satisfied desire strengthened. Two lives
become one from one, mobile and frozen.

Stand back to get a handle: ear-wear,
a thwarted O, an obeliskesque menhir
hollowed, a net to catch hope in,

the soul of the tree. A height-defying
pendulum case filleted and stilled.
A blown smoke ring lingering.

An opening, a gulley, a volley, a valley,
a closed loop, two-flanged and handsome,
an over-exerted escutcheon adjourned,

then plundered for shade, a long note
from an angel's throat once sung
can never be silenced. Your life outlined.

Grus Grus

When your mate stalks off in a huff
you need to make your mind up quick
if you wish to remain *in situ*
in haughtier disregard, or follow them —
for a grey crane's range is long,
and before you know it
they'll have gone too far for you to follow,
out beyond a particular edge of things.
Extremadura seems as good a place as any
to gather, faintly cocktail-tailed, toppling
about the grassland perfunctorily,
extraordinarily long necks overdangling
existentialist legs, collecting in dispersing groups
unsure which is the followed or the following.

Haiku na Feirme

1

catkins flattened
along the forest paths
spoor of spring quickening through

2

dust flies, clods dissolve, stones roll
harrows hop and heckle
over ploughed ground

3

marigold and celandine
hi-viz spatterings
on the marshland floor

4

sowed fields disclosing
a scrim of fresh green
warped drills wefting overhill

5

Aberdeen Angus in new grass
swatches of black suede
on bright green baize

6

bright tints fleck the verge
silage pinstripes the hill
our new spring wear is in

7

sly lover, the sun's first ray
slips through the gate bars
out onto the lane

8

how high can these buzzards fly
high summer, high noon
pinpricking the eye?

9

dusty cattle paths
unwind their worn desires
through empty pastureland

10

Páirc na Colúr at dusk
flashes of under-scut
smothered by burrows

11

combine's giant churning maw
bellyful of oats
straw loosely voiding

12

after the slow wisdom
of the wood pigeon
the jibber of a finch

13

swash, buckle and crunch
of Wellington boots
tramping over wet stubble

14

rough blusters shake down
the rowan, ruby jewels
rattle the tin roof

15

slurry freshly spread
and a squillion chortling starlings
pick their take

16

shrill whistles from stubble
lost pheasant chicks
echolocate each other

17

harshish raspings
from the Blind Island
crotchety snipe sharpen their knives

18

all snowflakes issue
from the same source eternally
as we go there

19

frost fossilizes fields and wood
locking the Pond Field Pond
rock solid

20

is it the wind crying
in the trees, or the trees
crying in the wind?

The Nightjar

If it was a dog I heard last night,
if that was your dog that you felt strangely
close to then (what it was doing out
at that hour we can explain somehow),
and if you were thinking at that precise time
about your father, mother, sister,
none granting you the permission you needed
to go,

if the nightjar belted like a flap-bell
past your window as a child such that you never
on nights like these can forget the fright,
if the still countryside at night
couldn't do as much for you
as the anxious hum of a big city
in the small hours, if the company

of trees never transferred in the genes,
or the ignition of fiction, if you could
never feel again that lifting free
of the time you both trailed the river
in the blue canoe, dragging it across fields
to the old railway line in the bog
beyond the woods below the house
you had to ignore to survive,

if freedom from here is also knowing
there's always home and welcome, but the pain
and its return has broken you
so as not to be able to bear the arrival,
and to what and for what — to descend again?

If this is and was all there is and was,
as something that could be light reveals
walls, blinds, ceiling, at least

one more darkness is gone for good,
and the nightjar may never return.

Encroachment

A tiger behind the dunes paces back and forth
in cover of she-oak, fuschia, thorn.

She is enraged by the sea wind,
the constancy of the waves,
glimpses of an expanse not yet hers.

I sit it out in the middle of the beach,
my back to the water, facing the lowering sun.
The fall of the surf along the curved strand behind
washes from one ear into the other.

Only those with few imperatives remain:
young lovers coiled on loose sand,
the elderly slumped in their chairs,
a teenager in a dark hoodie
waiting for the ocean to stage
its act of final destruction.

The breeze cools and I put my book down,
hearing at last the groans of hunger
from the running beast's stomach,
her swift pads quickening
like heartbeats across the sand.

At Sea

We walked across one strand
through unspeakable spoil
to the next and, suddenly —

out of nowhere — reed beds
right beside us, then
a river, brisk and fluent,

divulging our pre-Christmas
tryst. You stashed the shells
in your coat *au lait*, stone

all-sorts, a glass rhomb.
I still don't know for sure
where the river, if it really was,

empties into the ocean —
in so much of a tither
with everything yet to say.

After Ælfric

1 A MAN OF WINCHESTER

A man of Winchester
scolded his slave

for some small fault
and fettered him

in iron holds.
He hobbled off

to seek Saint Swithin
and petition him.

The holds flew open
and he ran free.

2 THE SPIRIT IS BY NATURE A TRINITY

The spirit is by nature a trinity
of memory, understanding and will,

yet one substantial whole —
one life, one substance, one spirit

of three distinct parts
which are separate

and yet, relative to other things,
maintain a unity in themselves:

I understand that which
I will to remember,

I will that which
I understand and remember,

and wherever memory is
there is always understanding and will.

3 LET US NOW CONSIDER THE SWIFTNESS OF SPIRIT

Let us now consider the swiftness of spirit.
It can heed heaven while quartering water.

Trek through kingdoms and cities, then dismiss
them all with a thought. At mention of a place

by name, imagine it — no matter where.
Revive by a word anything dead or alive

or dreamt; it's viable even in sleep. But while
pondering Rome it cannot evoke Jerusalem,

bearing in mind one thought only at a time,
the Almighty alone being mindful of all things.

Dan

My grandfather, my grandfather
whom I never knew, with all his heavy
responsibilities (which he eschewed),
holding me in his arms, as you might want
someone to, as my mother said he did,
his last year on Earth, his furrowed head,
fusty waistcoat, skinny tie, his genial eyes
and affection for her — her hard coming
to a house that couldn't be hers awhile,
his saying (I take no pride in this):
Ah Nan, he is the one, he is the one
who will be the making of us; look at him,
his genial eye, his how-do-you-do. Nan,
a stór, thank you. Thank you, Nan.

'The May Altar...'

was her birthright and her apotheosis.
Lilac, bluebell, a wild iris or two,
flurries of primroses

for the side aisles, and always some apple blossom
from the older trees —
lichen-stemmed, pinking into bloom

like the shrill sermons we would preach
while she was busy in the sacristy
up on tiptoe at the pulpit

reaching our arms into the scented air
and surprised by how easy it was
to flourish our words.

Lost Chorus

You'll never make it to there now,
even at the trees' thickest — the centre
extending outwards always to admit
new voices jugging, whooping, spilling,
the blackbird's surge, chaffinch's glissando,
and the alarm calls, love calls,
stay-off-my-patch calls — earnest,
fulsome, nothing just for the sake of it,
the undiminished mash-up needing no
appraisal as you forge onwards, inwards,
towards the earsplitting point of it all —
but fail, your need for climax appeased
by these rooks unhooding the canopy,
warm air's ease, stream's silvery trickle.

Long Distance

Standing on the front steps,
the sky still too bright for all the stars to shine,

I send one loud shout off into the valley
and in their own time, Clearagh, Mount Music,
Ardaneneen, all reply —

but then a pause,
a silence waiting for one last place

to answer. I must believe
this is the Universe
letting me know

that my call has been received
and logged and will
be dealt with in due course.

Crex Crex

My pedals creak against the hill
until I cannot believe my ears,
what I'm hearing, after all this time —

the bay seems far, but you are
here where I might touch your quick
cricketry grating: *ate mate, ate mate,*

ate mate, as my mother would say.
Unsure if this is a first encounter
or if her story has become mine

I dismount to survey thick meadow
set aside for your pleasure,
these sloping stone-walled acres

alive now with your surround
sound, switching off and on
as you quarter hidden ground

in an invisible chivvy, your upturned
gawp transmitting to the region —
sending word out for

the one woman in west Kerry
your line desperately depends on.

Working from Home

Traolach's roofers are at it again this morning,
their failing tattoos across the field
like an engine faltering.

Two swallows loop over the trees
trailing a stream of liquid song
that can only mean joy.

Gentle warmth rising,
the hum of the timber mill,
the low oceanic roar of the road.

Some grey crows pace the lawn
like a draught of butlers on their day off.

But I have work to do
to keep all this as it is:
remote, dishabited, ordinary.

Dreaming Seamus Heaney

1 A BAR OUT WEST

We step down from street level
into low lighting, long ceiling boards,
tweed and taste and well-shorn beards,

and you the instant faux-ignored
centre of attention, sizing it all up
and a wink in my direction

as if to say: *Stick at it,
keep going, don't mind them
and their notions of what should be.*

2 THE EAST WING

After the big speeches and poems
for the great homecoming

you and Marie held the table
with your well-tested harmonies.

Leaving, I drew you to Cooke's Irish Pike
but you were distracted, pressing me

in earnest: Do you ever want to get away?
I mean, away from it all?

Staring at your glass-reflected face,
All the time, I replied, all the time.

3   THE LONG HALL

Landing your pint on a beer mat
I asked you what you made
of the recent spate of memoirs from the poets.

You dropped the map you were reading,
raised your glass
and levelled your eyes with mine

saying:
Better not to mix your drinks —
I'm more of a grain than a grape man myself.

When you laughed
the gaps of your back teeth
made it seem more real.

4   A READING IN DUBLIN

The tall Nordic writer made great sense
and then no sense at all.

I knew it was out of keeping —
your grey hair braided in
a laurel wreath as you

paced up and down the steps
between the benches

preoccupied with a phrase
not yet in place,
playing your fingers
against an imaginary table.

5 STRANGE WORDS

I came to put a hand on this book,
feel its slim possibility,
smell the rot in the quires,
sow discord from authority.

You spoke this to me
as though saying it again —
who should never have to repeat anything —
so that my shame woke me.

6 DELICATESSE

The grey evening sky gave off a glow
that pewter-plated everything but the old apple tree.

Take it and eat it, you said, the flesh fructified
to a point where it becomes delectable.

The wood become meat, I broke it off
carefully in thumb-sized pieces.

Smelling of lamb or beef slow-cooked
over fire, jelly almost, hints of decay,

so sweet and gamey and now beyond taste
as it warmed my body entirely.

Observing all this you began to glow
with the old flesh-wisdom of that holy place.

7 THE FACE

You come in and sit at the kitchen table
to write blank-faced postcards.

You enquire again about my incident,
regret no poem came for the old Volks.

Now you are signing broadsheets and you ask
if I can take a photograph to send to them at home.

I angle the phone, but a light over your head
overexposes the scene.

Try what I might,
your face does not appear on the screen.

Steeplechase

Time galloping beside me,
a thoroughbred, fluid, easy — Arkle
alongside Mill Reef,
our shins brushing the fences,

our breaths one stream
spun and drawn
from chests silvered in sweat
as, flat out, we make and keep pace

pounding the turf, twin engines
of a life lived close together,
clearing the next fence abreast,
our last —

and you pull away from me,
eyes bright, rider clung
to your dark mane,
her glance back —

is that a smile? The whip
whirrs at my ear as I
fall behind your lithe haunches;
cheers rise, hats fly.

Vixen

Was it the lights of the village
on one end, making it bigger
and brighter than it could be
in the dead of Christmas night,
or the lit compound fog cloud
over the timber mill on the other;
or the hard still cold of the air,
the weir just audible

from the open front window
where we strained in wait
for each sharp searing shriek
echoing up to Clearagh and back,
as she ranged the lower fields
like a dream searching for its dreamer
criss-crossing the unseen
and mourning and weeping
in her dark valley of tears?

Anything

On the bridge at dusk
in either ear blackbird and thrush
belt out their routine.

Bats mob the sluggish flies,
their near swoops
soft cuffs of dark matter.

Tomorrow, two decades almost
to the day, you leave us
as you came: smiling, wise

to our flaws, ready always
to learn more about how
love can make anything happen.

Interval

You spoke the way people in the BBC aren't supposed to anymore. You'd spotted me exiting the security area, winging it, and inspected my credentials with great courtesy, smiling when I thanked you for taking good care of our safety. I knew you had the measure of my errand. Later by the canal as I leaned against a cable reel, you came up to me, eye to eye, and spoke to me in Korean, knowing I would understand. Your dark hair swept back and held tight, growing the bones of your face, your eyes comfortable in their place. You always preferred belted Macintoshes, even in winter. My sunroom was a triumph, you would say from the clapped-out ottoman, stretching in anticipation of love. I would nurse you through illness to a swift death, never knowing where in the capital you had lived, or anything else about your life.

Solstice

In or around now,
the sun's arc collapsed,
the days gone to nothing,

a beam will appear in the transom,
slip through the stained-glass shade
and snake along the wall as far as the clock;

a frail glow gilds the inner hall
until, like a trip switch thrown,
light and source expire behind Clearagh,

pitching us,
pale and squinting,
into a last dark night of the soul.

Oriole

Not oriel, or aureole —
Oriole. Exotic without going

tropical, your throaty ease
befits gold velure,

a tatty sawn-off jacket, beak
to pierce an earling. Oriole

of Deia fluting through
our hot nights from its Aleppo

in the valley. Orioles
of Goleen and Baltimore

returning in our sleep
to steal a space

between their phrases:
oriolus, riolus, olus, us.

Strobus

Your adoption day, planting a tree
in the Shedfield ditch to succeed
the large declining sycamore,

my spade strikes metal and I pull
from a tangle of briar and ivy
the frame of your first bike, rubber grips
split and faded, pedals still turning —

and then up comes a toy phone
that you or someone else discarded,
its keypad legible still,
the convex screen expectant.

I raise it, caked with earth, to my cheek
wanting to leave you a voicemail
that explains where all the years have gone.

Artisan

Autumn plumps
every fruit and seed,

glosses each
with a fingertip —

and none more so
than these:

the lacquered nipples
of the rose hip.

The Miller

After that there appeared
to them the upper body
of an ugly big belligerent

fire-blackened miller,
hoiking all he could
of valuables and goods —

cattle even — into the wide
open mouth of his mill.
What are you up to, man?

they asked. I'll tell you,
he replied, anything of this world
that's the subject of a grudge

I toss in here, to the maw
of my mill — because I am
the Miller from Hell

who grinds all your gall away.

Athairne

Before I was born my mother
craved a mouthful of ale, but was refused.

I called from the womb
at the despicable brewer who denied us:

'For the sake of a draught of ale,
all from one woman's rage

lightning will lash at the tide
and the sea will smother the Earth

bursting all dams like nuts cracking;
barrels will break their hoops,

flooding the place with ale, so that
you will have to wade through your own

house while my mother scoops
three sweet handfuls to her mouth.'

Whenever refused a drink
be in no doubt that any poet will hole

your hogsheads with his words
and not leave a single drop behind.

Haus Sonas

From the room with a view up towards Schmittenhöhe
we watch each morning for the cable cars to start.
Like strung glass beads they'll move at nine
into smooth slow motion down and up the slopes,
steady in their passage over woods and pistes
with wildflowers for the grazing cows to chew.
I mark a point where two cars meet: the cable is
invisible from here, so it feels miraculous each time
they draw close, eclipse, then re-emerge, each one
emboldened on its adverse trajectory. What can we
learn from our floating steel and glass mobiles?
That constancy is love's best chance? Or that
there's no meaning to our presence here on Earth,
except what we can engineer from happenstance?

Byrd

Discovery, proof it exists,
appearing first as a shadow
that diffuses like smoke
in light falling along
thin shafts to reveal
an infinitely delicate minute
creature, veined wings shy
of a lucent core, neck and head
and pin-beak barely visible
as it lifts and hovers. Incredulous
at my good luck, my passage
into vision, I raise an arm slowly,
stretch an index finger, and so
it traverses the air, wings hidden
in rapid beat, unsettling no
dust motes, and settles
on my skin, digs sharp talons in,
its sole defence. Resting,
it fixes a tiny diamond eye on mine,
then tightens its grip. I cry out
and it vanishes, my first byrd.

Excursion

1

As we walked down to Natural Bridge
the water filling the crystal pool
sent thunder up to our steep descent,
drowning the birdsong, and our voices too,
so you could only signal your surprise
at coming to the opening of the cave
where the glow-worms grow their gauzy skies
and once the Kombumerri crouched for shade.
But all my thought then was in the past,
back along the path with the giant fig
which, having colonized and held his host
for centuries in tight embrace, reneged
and snugly strangled her, the very tree
he'd relied on most to reach the canopy.

2

Later on, out at The Spit, from huge cubed
boulders like thrown dice, abandoned toys,
extending your continent by a few
feet more into the Coral Sea and pausing
the endless beach in neat parenthesis,
we watched the wind-afflicted water
toss and pitch a dredger offshore from us.
I couldn't square those solid blocks
cast for a useful new promontory
with their rain-gouged basalt counterparts
at Natural Bridge: how *off* they seemed,
poor forgeries of an ancient art
just as beneath the Border Ranges, lies
your gaudy, pop-up Surfers Paradise.

3

There wasn't much to say, watching the haul
of tuna slowly disload fish by fish
from a trawler, as we ate our sea-spoils
on the quay in heat that brought a whiff
of fuel and guts up from the landing place.
Each sunburned, bare-topped sailor
pulled one from the hold which he'd embrace
and heft club-footed up the deck to weigh
on the bloodied hook. How calmly
we surveyed the wholly indefensible.
A pelican floated in, then sagely
left again in search of better spectacle.
You asked if I was ready to return
and scattered our leftovers to the gulls.

Such a Thing

This boy
was going sowing

oats, and his
father quizzed

him. How much
will you put

to the acre?
Two hundred,

said the boy.
You'll never do,

his father said,
you must sow

four grains
for one to grow:

one for the rat,
one for the crow,

one for to rot,
and one for to grow.

Our Journey

Ferns and greying
fireweed fall
sodden and exhausted

narrowing to a path
the roadway
we two walk

in the failing light
of early autumn
in our lives.

On McAllister Street

You didn't need to tell me the room
had not been visited or the bed slept in for years.
I could feel it in the sheets, marble
cold underneath, stone wadding
of the bolster. And in the sleep that came and left
through the night, a tireless questioning
until a weak glow leaked through the blinds
promising memory and everything revealed
to the portraits on the dressing table and walls —
Irish and Jewish faces where only the children
smiled. How strange to see a bride alone,
bouquet held aside like a parchment.
She, like you, dark and radiant, her train
arranged around her feet like frozen snow.

Caption

It is impossible for any man
to describe the sad and melancholy state
of hunger, sickness, despair, and death.

The landed proprietors within ten
or twelve miles are absentees,
so the people have nowhere else to turn.

Our people are dying in the streets,
on the roads, and in the houses,
some left for four, six, seven days without interment,
without winding sheets.

It is frightful to behold children dying
and crying for food
and none to be got without money
and no money to be had.

Afforestation

On the evening of the day before it happened
Traolach and I walked home from Lissarda.
Our talk was of trees, ash dieback, past elms —
but not without a strong disagreement
on the value of the plantation at Ballymichael,
its prime function financial, how bare and cold
it is inside, how it has smothered the spirits
of the fields and those who worked in them,
O'Mahonys mainly; and, having backtracked
so he could show me two diverse redwoods,
and reviewing what is planned by the new owners
of the land between the river and the road,
we agreed — there is majesty, sure enough,
in that green sweep, peaks along the skyline.

On Reaching Heng Mountain

Each time I made it to a new peak
I found that you had been there already
to say how well the cascades
thread the far green slopes with silver.
You left no words for me to use.

Still, I followed as you showed the way
along the river path under a changing moon
through folds of wisteria and vine entwined.
You would slip peach blossom into my belt as I went,
bid a toast always — always a warm goodbye.

Now, like your friend Li Tuan,
no longer *Collator of the Books,*
I leave behind Hangzhou and its daily grind,
tune the old lute to a new scale,
find my own song up here on Heng — at last!

Acknowledgements and Notes

A number of poems are dedicated to the following people: 'Haus Sonas' is in memory of Anne Crowley, 'On McAllister Street' is for Sherrie Matza and Joe O'Donoghue, 'Back from a night cycle . . . ' is for Nicholas, 'Nursery Rhymes' is for James, 'Thornflower' is for Theo Dorgan, 'Return to Coolea' is for Peadar Ó Riada, 'After Ælfric' is for Éamonn Ó Carragáin. 'The May Altar . . .' is in memory of my mother Nan (Howard) FitzGerald. 'Crex Crex' is for John O'Halloran, 'Anything' is for Elena, 'Strobus' is for Alexander, 'Caption' is for John Crowley and 'On Reaching Heng Mountain' is for Greg Delanty.

'Lauriston' first appeared in *On the Banks: Cork City in Poems and Songs*, edited by Alannah Hopkin, (Collins Press, Cork, 2016). 'Grus Grus' first appeared in *Festschrift for Gerry Murphy*, privately published by Southword Editions (Cork 2022). *Haiku na Feirme* first appeared as a limited letterpress edition published by Jamie Murphy of The Salvage Press (Dublin, 2021). 'Vixen' first appeared in a limited letterpress edition made in collaboration with artist Dorothy Cross entitled *Darklight*, also published by Jamie Murphy of The Salvage Press (Dublin, 2021). 'Solstice' first appeared on display in FitzGerald's Park, Cork, in 2021 as part of the Cork City Libraries' *Poetry in the Park* Collection.

page 27   'Wounded Angel' is inspired by a painting of the same name by Hugo Simberg at the Ateneum Art Museum, Helsinki.

page 28   The Gobelins Manufactory (Manufacture des Gobelins) is a renowned tapestry and textile factory in Paris established by the Gobelin family in the fifteenth century and best known for supplying the courts of the French monarchs since Louis XIV. It is still active.

page 36   'Before You Speak' is a response to the poem 'After you Speak' by Edward Thomas.

page 38   'Magnus Modus' is inspired by a sculpture of the same title by Joseph Walsh at the National Gallery of Ireland.

page 48   'After Ælfric' is based on a set of Old English sermons on Saints' Days collected as *Ælfric's Lives of Saints* edited by Walter W Skeat (OUP, 1966).

pp 68/69 'The Miller' and Athairne' are based on translated extracts from the Old Irish texts *Immram Curaig Úa Corra* and *Bretha Nemed Déidenach* respectively.

page 72 The Kombumerri are an indigenous people of the Nerang region of Northern Queensland, Australia.

page 74 This poem is based on an entry recorded by Kilmurry National School, County Cork, in the Irish National Folklore Commission Schools' Collection circa 1937 (Vol 0340, p.178).

page 77 'Caption' is based on a petition for relief to the Lord Lieutenant of Ireland written in 1847 by Peter Ward, Parish Priest of Partry, County Mayo, and recorded in the Famine Distress Papers at the National Archives of Ireland (D5749). The source was located and transcribed by Breandán Ó Cíobháin.